THE BATTLE FOR YOUR MIND

NAHUM ROSARIO

Maranatha Publications
Chicago, Illinois

The Battle for Your Mind

Copyright © 2001, Nahum Rosario

All Rights Reserved. No part of this publication may be reproduced, stored in a retrieval system or transmitted in any form or by any means – electronic, mechanical, photocopy, recording or any other – except for brief quotations in printed reviews, without the prior permission of the author.

All Scripture quotations, unless otherwise specified, are from the *Authorized King James Version* of the Bible.

Published originally in Spanish with the title *La Batalla por Tu Mente*. English Translation by: Laudir J. Lugo.

Cover design by Rogelio Guzmán ©
Cover Illustration protected by the 1976 United States Copyright Act

Printed in Canada by
Essence Communications Group Belleville, Ontario

ISBN: 1-930115-03-2

**For more information or
to order additional copies, please contact:**

Maranatha Publications
4301 W. Diversey Ave. Chicago, IL 60639 USA
(773) 384-7717 • www.maranathachicago.com

This book is dedicated to all of the pastors of MARANATHA WORLD REVIVAL MINISTRIES whom are fighting "the good fight of faith" in order to set the minds of men and women free from the influence of Satan and the spirit of this age. I pray this book would be of great inspiration to you as well as to every minister of the gospel of Jesus Christ. May it also help spiritual leaders as they wrestle to raise up a new generation that thinks the marvelous thoughts of God and which has the mind of Christ.

Contents

Introduction. 7

1. Who Controls Your Mind?. 9

2. The States of the Mind. 19

3. The Renewal of the Mind. 29

4. Tearing Down Strongholds. 47

5. The Power of Thinking 63

6. Thinking God's Thoughts 73

7. A New Mentality 83

Introduction

Something that the Holy Spirit is awakening in the Church is the awareness of the kind of spiritual warfare that believers engage in. All over the world there seems to be an emphasis on spiritual warfare. As a result of this, Christians are assuming a militant position in their spiritual lives. We've realized that *"we wrestle not against flesh and blood, but against principalities against powers, against the rulers of darkness of this world, against spiritual wickedness in high places"* (Ephesians 6:12).

We can truly say that the Church has moved from a defensive position, to an offensive position. There has been a change in the spiritual world, which has been received by Christians and churches that desire to move with God and conquer everything that rightfully belongs to us by faith. The church of this new century will be a Church that will possess the gates of its enemies and will cast down the accuser of the brethren.

The purpose of this book isn't to discuss the battle that we will fight against Satan and his demons in the heavenly realms. It is purposed to deal with the battle that is fought every minute in the minds and consciousness of individuals. This book was birthed in me as a result of my observations in this area and by some words that the Holy Spirit impressed in my spirit. As we experienced a period of warfare and spiritual conflict in the church that I pastor; I heard the following words in my spirit: *"My people are losing the battle in their war against their enemies in the heavenly realms, because they still haven't won the battle in their minds."* It was then that I realized that Believers can not win the battle in the heavenly realm until they destroy and conquer the strongholds that Satan has erected in their own minds.

We're living in a day in which a deadly battle for the soul of humanity is being fought. According to the Scriptures and to what we're seeing occur in society, we conclude that we're living in the last days of the history of the human race. Satan knows that the time when he and his fallen angels will be cast eternally into the lake of fire is near, so in the mean time he wants to deceive and control as many people as he can. One of his greatest tactics is to control the minds of people, so they can become his spiritual robots and thus do his will. But, I have good news for you; God has made provision for you to win this war with the spiritual weapons He has provided for us in Christ. Prepare for victory in the name of Jesus.

In the service of my Lord Jesus,

Chapter One

Who Controls Your Mind?

"Your mind can be the workshop of God or the workshop of Satan, depending on who spends more time working in it."

In my contacts and conversations with thousands of Christians; I've often taken notice of the conflicts and problems that come against them and that hinder them from fully realizing their God given spiritual potential. These individuals have experienced authentic conversions and are truly born-again. However, they fail to demonstrate stability in their spiritual lives. Some excuse themselves shifting the blame to the devil or even to other people; while others have resorted to a spiritual life that is like a roller coaster, one day up and the next day down.

Part of this problem has to do with the fact that it has been thought that the only important thing in the life of a believer is the condition of their spirit, and that everything else just fixes it self or just falls into place. This just isn't so. The Bible speaks of our salvation as a work that affects the three areas of the human being: the spirit, the soul and the body.

> *"And the very God of peace sanctify you wholly; and I pray God your whole spirit and soul and body be preserved blameless unto the coming of our Lord Jesus Christ"* (1 Thessalonians 5:23).

Love the Lord with all Your Mind

> *"And thou shalt love the Lord thy God with all thy heart, and with all thy soul, and with all thy mind, and with all thy strength: this is the first commandment"* (Mark 12:30).

One day as I meditated on that verse, I was impacted by the phrase "with all thy mind." Until that moment, it hadn't occurred to me that God not only wanted me to love Him with all of my soul, but also with my entire mind. Therefore the condition or state of my mind must be important to God. This is true, because it is the mind that thinks, analyzes, reasons, remembers and memorizes. It is these activities of the mind that hinder people from serving and loving God when that mind is not surrendered to the Lord. We can never progress spiritually, unless our minds are in harmony with God.

Of all the beings created, man is the only one that has the ability to think, because he was the only one created in the image and likeness of God. This is why he has the ability to decide, choose and has a free will. It is no secret that the thing that God gave man to serve and worship Him with, has become the major obstacle keeping man from knowing and enjoying all of the blessings that God wishes to bestow upon him.

What I just finished saying isn't only for the heathen or unbelievers. It is also for Christians that want to try to live a new life with an old mind, which is at enmity with God. If we desire to fulfill the first and greatest commandment of God, we've got to pay attention to the state of our mind. It is impossible to love the Lord with your whole mind; if part of it is not yet submitted totally to His will. We can apply the words of the Apostle James to those individuals: *"A double minded man is unstable in all his ways"* (James 1:8). The inconsistency that we see in spiritual lives of so many Christians is a result of a double mind, which is split between trying to please God and communion with the world.

We Were Enemies in the Mind

"And you, that were sometime alienated and enemies in your mind by wicked works, yet now hath he reconciled" (Colossians 1:21).

Paul clearly tells us that before we were saved our minds were at enmity with God and led us to wicked works that totally separated us from God. The problem with the sinner is not what he does, but what he thinks, because what he does is a result of what he first thought. This has in reality been the condition of man since he first sinned in Eden. It was for this reason that God repented for even creating man. The Bible declares:

"And God saw that the wickedness of man was very great in the earth, and that the every imagination of the

THE BATTLE FOR YOUR MIND

thoughts of his heart was only evil continually" (Genesis 6:5).

Though we've been reconciled with God through the blood of His Son Jesus, we can still say that there are often thoughts that tend to live a life apart from God. Even though we're saved, the data of experiences, habits and memories of our past lives battle within us to control us and keep us at enmity with God.

If we desire to please God, there's going to have to be a change in our behavior and in our way of thinking. According to Ephesians 2:3, we were children of wrath because we fulfilled the desires of the flesh and of the mind. We ought to understand that the flesh can desire nothing unless it first receives a command from the mind to desire. Therefore a sinner has no choice but to be a slave to his thoughts, because he is totally separated from the life of God. The Believer has the advantage of being able to control his thoughts, because he has three means that provide the ability to do it; the life of God, the Word of God and the Holy Spirit.

A Believer that doesn't take advantage of those means will live a miserable life, because he will never fully enjoy communion with God. If the mind is not in communion with God, it is at friendship with the world. This poses a great problem for Believers, for the Bible is extreme in its position concerning this matter and clearly tells us:

> *"Ye adulterers and adulteresses, know ye not that the friendship of the world is enmity with God? Whosoever therefore will be a friend of the world is the enemy of God"* (James 4:4).

Who Controls Your Mind?

I don't want to be caught in the fix of being a child of God while at the same time being His enemy. To avoid this, let us make a decision to do something with our mind so that our mind might be reconciled with God just as our spirit is.

The Mind on Things from Above

"If ye then be risen with Christ, seek those things which are above, where Christ sitteth on the right hand of God. Set your affection on things above, not on things on the earth" (Colossians 3:1-2).

God expects an individual that is born-again to set his mind on the things of the Spirit. According to Paul the reason for this is that we have risen with Christ. It is the resurrection power that is within us which gives us the ability to redirect our sight or minds towards the things of God. The Bible doesn't suggest that we set our minds on things above. It commands us to set our minds on things above.

In this letter Paul is correcting the Christians at Colosse whom thought that they could control the appetites of the flesh by means of human rules (Colossians 2:20-23). It is this kind of teaching that has caused frustration and defeat in the lives of thousands of Christians that try to have victory in the flesh without first renewing their minds by the Word of God.

The path towards victory begins when an individual knows and understands that they've received a greater life, which enables him to transfer his thoughts from earthly things to heavenly things. It is only then that we can discover the treasures of the life of Jesus, which are

purpose of life

hidden in God. It is humanly impossible to understand this truth unless we determine to change our priorities and put the Kingdom of God first in our lives. It all begins with a decision to begin thinking thoughts that are in agreement with God's purpose for our lives.

It is useless trying to control the desires and impulses of the flesh, without first taking control of the thoughts that activate our flesh. The Bible declares, *"As a man thinketh in his heart so is he"* (Proverbs 23:7) implying the following. Whoever has control of your mind will end up controlling your whole being. God's greatest commandment to us is to love Him with all of our heart (spirit), soul, mind and strength. It is God's will for us to experience an entire salvation, in which our whole being is sanctified and separated to serve the Lord.

A Better Covenant

> *"For this covenant that I will make with the house of Israel after those days, saith the Lord; I will put my laws into their minds and write them in their hearts: and I will be to them a God, and they shall be to me a people"* (Hebrews 8:10).

Today we live under a new covenant, which was instituted through the death and resurrection of our Lord Jesus Christ. This covenant is superior to the one that Moses received on Mt. Sinai, because it promises a radical transforming in the life of whoever receives it. We see in the previous scripture that this covenant is effective to the extent that an individual allows God to put His laws in their mind. Notice how important it is to receive the Word of God in the mind so that it can be written in the heart. Remember this, God won't do anything in your life that you don't allow Him to. When you decide to put the Word first in your life, then God will put it in your mind and write it in your heart.

If we can understand this awesome promise of God we will realize that God is seeking a people that will walk in the power and authority of this new covenant. Even though we're saved through this covenant, we must go deeper into it receiving the words and promises of this covenant in our hearts and minds. When we begin to take this seriously, Satan's dominion will begin to crumble in our minds and we'll serve God in the new life of the Spirit. Don't forget! God will keep His part of the covenant, if you keep yours.

God longs to establish a special relationship with us, where we can see Him as our personal God and enjoy all of the blessings that Jesus purchased for us at the cross of Calvary. Now do you understand the importance of having our minds under the control and authority of God?

Satan Wants Your Mind

If you'd ask people, who has your mind? They would all answer the same; I do. Both Believers and sinners believe that they can have absolute dominion of their minds without any external intervention. Ever since Eden, Satan has used this thinking to deceive men into thinking that they can be like God. That man can be good or bad without the outside influence of God or the devil is a premise of humanism. Stemmed from this reasoning comes the teaching that bad or good is nothing more than a state of mind, and that it can be treated by positively affirming the good that resides in every person.

This may sound pretty, but it's not what God's Word

teaches. According to the Apostle John, the whole world along with its culture, philosophy, politics, economy and religion is under the control of wickedness (1 John 5:19). It is no secret that Satan, who is the God of this world and the prince of the power of the air, is in a continual competition with God to control the spirits, minds and bodies of human beings. It may not be popular to say this, but its reality. The devil and his demons have control in these three areas of individuals, which don't serve God in spirit and in truth.

Maybe you're a born-again Christian and you've asked yourself, could it be possible that Satan can have influence in my life even though I'm a Believer in the Lord Jesus Christ? There are two proofs to verify this, the Word of God and the daily experience of millions of Christians around the world.

Many Christians live in a spiritual fantasy where they think that if they ignore the devil that he will in turn ignore them, but that's not reality. If there's anyone that Satan wants to oppress and destroy it's the children of God, because that is how he tries to put God to shame. Since the devil can't mess with God, he settles for those that are dearest to God's heart, the children He purchased with the blood of Jesus. Let's not be ignorant of the fact that Satan has a plan to attack Christians in every area of life.

Let us be mindful that Satan cannot enter into the spirit of a Christian, but he can bombard him from the outside to depress and weaken him. Not only can the mind be oppressed, but Satan can also occupy it in strategic locations. That is why Paul admonishes us with the following: *"Give no place to the devil"* (Ephesians 4:27), and James

Who Controls Your Mind?

adds: *"Resist the devil and he will flee from you"* (James 4:7). Satan knows that unless a Christian renounces his faith in Jesus Christ, he cannot enter into his spirit. Since the devil knows he lost dominion over the Believer's spirit, he makes the mind his favorite target of attack.

The enemy knows the functioning of the human mind all too well and he knows that if he can keep his stronghold in the mind of a Believer, four things will occur:

1. The renewed spirit of the individual will not have liberty of expression.
2. The individual will have no peace in their relationship and communion with God.
3. The mind will be an instrument to cause the flesh to sin.
4. There will be no spiritual authority to fight against the works of the devil.

Now do you realize the importance of understanding the functioning of the mind of a born-again individual? The mind is the foremost battleground for a child of God and that is where his victory or defeat, holiness or sinfulness, healing or sickness is determined. It is a spiritual reality or truth that whoever has most territory and time in your mind is the one that has control for the advantage of his kingdom. You make the decision, whether it will be God or the devil.

Why Do I Have Struggles?

This is one of the many questions that sincere individuals that desire to serve the Lord ask themselves when they find out that the Christian's life is not always a bed

THE BATTLE FOR YOUR MIND

of roses. Many times people that couldn't get this decided to drop out of God's service, because Satan convinced them that they weren't saved, and that if they were they wouldn't be struggling so much.

This book is not intended to give glory to the devil or to make you afraid, but it is to make you aware of the importance of renewing, sanctifying and leading your mind towards victory. Remember this, God has not made provision for any Believer to live in defeat. You can be victorious in *The Battle for Your Mind,* because God designed you to win. In the next chapter you will discover the different states of the human mind, which will help you to understand the importance of a mind that has been delivered from the power of Satan and that will be an instrument to think God's thoughts. God wants each of His children to have a mind that will be free from all satanic influence and to have a mind that He can use to think His own thoughts.

Chapter Two

The States of the Mind

"Oh let the wickedness of the wicked come to an end; but establish the just; for the righteous God trieth the hearts (minds) and reigns" (Psalm 7:9).

"I the Lord search the heart (mind), I try the reins, even to give every man according to his ways, and according to the fruit of his doings" (Jeremiah 17:10).

Not many people are aware of the fact that God knows the exact state and condition of each individual. No matter what state your mind is in, God knows it. As well as knowing it, His Word also gives us the solution for putting man's mind in order, but first we have to clearly understand what God says in His Word concerning our state of mind (the Believer's and the Unbeliever's).

In the previous chapter we established the importance of knowing whether God or Satan is controlling your mind very clearly. Every sincere Christian wants to please God in everything they think, say and do. How many times have Christians that truly love the Lord found themselves doing things they didn't intend to do, which bring them guilt and condemnation? Part of the problem is the Believer's lack of revelation on this subject of the mind of the Believer. Getting saved doesn't solve all of our problems, but it enables us to face and overcome them by the grace of God.

The following section of this book is very important, because it will show you what our minds were like before getting saved. You will realize how certain trains of thought from the old mind still affect our minds today.

Each person has a different state of mind, depending on the depths of corruption that they may have sunken to. We can't deny that the time it will take for an individual's mind to be renewed, so that it can do God's will, is dependent upon the depths and lifestyle of sin and how long they were in that state of sin. The progress of spiritual development depends on those issues as well. We can't expect an individual that has lived a lifestyle of sin for 40 years to change in the same amount of time that someone that served the devil only 5 years will. This book will help new Believers, but it will also help those that have served the Lord for many years to be more patient with spiritual babies.

1 - The Reprobate Mind

reject God's knowledge.

> "And even as they did not like to retain God in their knowledge, God gave them over to a reprobate mind, to do those things which are not convenient" (Romans 1:28).

According to the Scripture, a reprobate mind is a result of rejecting the knowledge of God. Any person that has heard the Word of God and over and over again due to the hardness of their heart rejects it can reach this very dangerous state.

If we carefully read the first chapter of Romans, we will see that the sinful and shameful state or outcome of the individuals described in verse 18 through verse 32 is a result of a reprobate mind. A reprobate mind is nothing more than a mind abandoned by God, where the person loses all fear of God and His established laws of conduct found in the Ten Commandments. The person reached this mental state because, they wouldn't accept the truth, and they gave no glory to God and exchanged the truth of God for a lie.

We can conclude that this is the Western state of mind. A culture or an individual that has never heard of God cannot have a reprobate mind, because they have no knowledge of God. If we examine the uprising of sins that are currently "in style" or applauded by the affluent of our society we will realize that they are the same sins that Paul mentions in Romans 1. They are results of reprobate minds that have intentionally rejected the morality and righteousness of God's Word.

This is probably the reason why it is so difficult to convince a homosexual or a lesbian that what they are doing is out of the divine order of things, indecent and immoral. There was a time when even the world considered this type of conduct to be something abnormal and immoral. How then can we explain that certain so called Christians defend these lifestyles as an alternative to that which God clearly established in His Word from the beginning? Let us accept the answer for this behavior once and for all. God has had enough of these people and because they wouldn't accept His truth, He gave them over to a reprobate mind to do things, which are not convenient.

We Believers must be careful not to reject the knowledge of God and begin exchanging God's truth for a lie, as it seems convenient. I believe that nobody reaches the state of a reprobate mind overnight, but it was a slow process of disobedience and resistance to the Word and truth of God. I believe that this is the condition of an apostate. He didn't consider God. He obstructed the truth with injustice, changed the truth little by little for a lie, and he gave no glory to God. God deliver us from this dangerous state!

2 - The Darkened Mind

> *"This I say therefore, and testify in the LORD, that ye henceforth walk not as other Gentiles walk, in the vanity of their mind, Having the understanding darkened, being alienated from the life of God through the ignorance that is in them, because of the blindness of their heart: Who being past feeling have given themselves over unto lasciviousness, to work all uncleanness with greediness"* (Ephesians 4:17-19).

There is a basic difference between the reprobate mind and the darkened mind. The difference is that the darkened mind is a result of the absence of the life of God in an individual, which produces ignorance and hardness of heart. In his letter to the Ephesians, Paul warns them not to walk as the other Gentiles who have darkened minds do.

A darkened mind is a mind in obscurity. Every sinner has this type of mind, because they are dead in their trespasses and sins. Only the light of the Gospel can change this kind of mind. In another scripture Paul gives us the reason for this: *"In whom the god of this world hath blinded the minds of them which believe not, lest the light of the glori-*

ous gospel of Christ, who is the image of God, should shine unto them" (2 Corinthians 4:4). Darkness in the minds and hearts of unbelieving people is a result of satanic influence and the absence of the life of God within them.

In contrast to the reprobate mind, which rejected the knowledge and revelation that it once had of God, the darkened mind never had such knowledge or revelation. If we can grasp this, we will understand why it is easier for someone with a darkened mind to be changed than someone with a reprobate mind. In a sense, God will judge the person with a reprobate mind more severely than He would someone with a darkened mind.

According to Paul's letter to the Ephesians, it is possible for even Christians to walk in the vanity of a darkened mind. If that weren't true he wouldn't have warned of it in Ephesians 4:17-19. We must understand that even though we are Christians, there are still dark areas in our minds. The cure for this is the life of God and knowledge of His Word. This is why a believer should not remain ignorant of the light of the Word, that is, if he wants to live victoriously over sin, which is a result of a vain and darkened mind.

3 - The Carnal Mind

> *"Because the carnal mind is enmity against God: for it is not subject to the law of God, neither indeed can be"* (Romans 8:7).

The carnal mind is the mind that is controlled and manipulated by the physical and emotional part of the human being, that being the body and the soul. The Christian, who hasn't renewed his mind with the Word of God, is operating in a carnal mind. Even though this person may have experienced an authentic salvation experience, he hasn't learned to submit his mind to his renewed spirit, so that he can manifest the life and character of Jesus to the world. What determines whether a Christian is carnal is the state of his mind.

We said at the beginning of this book that the acts of the flesh in a Believer are a direct result of the state of his carnal mind. A person is carnal, because he spends the majority of the time thinking carnal things. Why does he think on carnal things? Because he hasn't set his mind on the things above, he hasn't been filled with the Word of God, and he hasn't allowed the Holy Spirit to take absolute control of his life.

Let's not forget that for many years our minds were conditioned to satisfy the desires of our flesh and souls. Now that we are saved, the conflict is greater because Satan knows that the things that he deposited in us are still stored up in our minds. He knows that he can use those things to get us to end up doing his will. This causes the carnal minded person to be at enmity with God, because he isn't doing God's will, and he maintains friendship with the world through his thoughts and the things he does.

> *"Ye adulterers and adulteresses, know ye not that the friendship of the world is enmity with God? Whosoever therefore will be a friend of the world is the enemy of God"* (James 4:4).

It's no wonder Paul tells us in Romans 8:6 that the person with a carnal mind is under the effects of spiritual death, even if he does call himself a son of God. The reason why he cannot submit to the law of God is because to do so the law of the Spirit of life in Christ Jesus must control his mind. The carnal mind responds to the flesh and emotions of the individual, instead of responding to the resurrected spirit that resides in each born-again individual.

The Bible tells us that we can identify a person with a carnal mind by several attitudes that they manifest in their conduct. One of these is pride or arrogance. In his letter to the Colossians, Paul warns them to be careful not to operate with a carnal mind. A carnally minded person will use their supernatural experiences to make themselves superior to other Believers. Paul says that a carnal mind puffs up and makes a person proud, and it hinders that person from receiving the spiritual blessings. He gives us advice and admonishment that is still good for today:

"Let no man beguile you of your reward in a voluntary humility and worshipping of angels, intruding into those things which he hath not seen, vainly puffed up by his fleshly mind" (Colossians 2:18).

Every time you see someone with a spirit of pride or superiority, they are operating with a carnal mind.

It is this pride that leads the person to show another characteristic of his spiritual life. Without a shadow of a doubt, the Christian with a carnal and puffed up mind always serves as an instrument for division within the life of the church. In my comprehensive pastoral experience, I've noticed that the people who create division and dissension within churches are those that think they're more spiritual and more anointed than the pastor himself. When you converse with these individuals you immediately find out that they're puffed up by pride, which is the manifestation of a carnal mind. Paul understood this all too well, that is why he told the church at Corinth without holding back, that they were carnal and in the flesh.

"For ye are yet carnal: for whereas there is among you envying, and strife, and divisions, are ye not carnal, and walk as men?" (1 Corinthians 3:3).

It has often been preached that only Christians who commit adultery, get drunk, and lie have carnal minds, but preachers have forgotten there are Christians who would never think of doing these things, yet they are still carnal. Why is this? The answer is they don't walk in love, peace and harmony with the other members of the Body of Christ.

4 - The Defiled Mind

"Unto the pure all things are pure: but unto them that are defiled and unbelieving is nothing pure; but even their mind and conscience is defiled" (Titus 1:15).

The meaning of the word "defiled" denotes the idea of something stained, violated, or dishonored. The Bible doesn't provide many details concerning a defiled mind, it only mentions it in one passage where it is established that a pure person cannot have a defiled mind. What is a defiled mind? According to Webster's New World Dictionary of the American Language (New Revised Expanded Pocket Size Edition, David B. Guralnik, Editor in Chief, Warner Books, New York, NY 10103, 1983) "to defile" means "to alter, make rot, pervert, thwart, seduce, and damage."

If we use the word in the context that Paul did, we have to conclude that there are some Christians with a defiled mind. Paul exhorts them to be pure in the faith, so that they don't have this kind of mind. These kinds of people have allowed their minds and conscience to be thwarted and perverted by this world's system. In these cases we can say that there has been a demonic seduction, which has defiled their minds. Even though these people call themselves Christians,

> *"They profess that they know God; but in works they deny him, being abominable, and disobedient, and unto every good work reprobate"* (Titus 1:16).

Satan has seduced a defiled mind, and it defiles every kind of thought. We can say that individuals with this kind of mind are impure, because they always judge or reason according to their condition. This person always sees impure and bad intentions in other people, because he thinks everyone is like him. This defiled mind is what causes them to become incredulous and cynical.

The root of a defiled mind is a defiled conscience. Your conscience is the voice of your spirit, and it is what accuses or approves our conduct, when it isn't defiled. If we mess up our conscience by ignoring it over and over, there can come a time when it will no longer convict us when we do what is wrong. This is why; if we desire to have a mind that is pure we should obey our conscience and allow the blood of Jesus to cleanse our conscience from every dead work. Every dead work that isn't cleansed by the blood and the Holy Spirit will bring defilement to our consciences and minds. That explains the behavior of certain so-called Christians, which feel no type of conviction even when they're in total rebellion against the LORD. These people end up being reprobate and fail in their attempt to serve God.

5 - The Spiritual Mind

> *"For they that are after the flesh do mind the things of the flesh; but they that are after the Spirit the things of*

the Spirit. For to be carnally minded is death; but to be spiritually minded is life and peace" (Romans 8:5-6).

It is the perfect will of God for every Christian to operate with the mind of the Spirit, so that we can please God. We stated before that we can not please God with a carnal state of mind. I think it is very important as children of God that we please our Father. Every father feels fulfilled and happy when his children try to please him. The Bible talks about two kinds of people that don't please God: those who don't live by faith (Hebrews 11:6) and those whose minds are after the things of the flesh (Romans 8:8). If we combine these two thoughts we can conclude that we can't live by faith without a spiritual mind. Do you see how important it is to have a spiritual mind?

We can also say that a spiritual mind is one that is controlled by the Holy Spirit. This is not direct control, because our mind has to be submitted to our born-again spirit. Within each Christian there is a conflict for control of our minds. On one side, the flesh fights for the mind to submit to its desires and on the other the reborn spirit (where Jesus now lives) fights for the mind to submit to its desires, so that we can be in harmony with the Creator that we might do His will.

Every Christian has to decide whether he will live according to the flesh or the Spirit. This decision will determine your progress and spiritual maturity. A spiritual mind will be the result of your absolute dedication to being wise and dedicating all of your energy to the things of the Spirit. This is the only way that you will enjoy an abundant life, which is full of righteousness, peace, and joy.

Chapter Three

The Renewal of the Mind

"And be not conformed to this world: but be ye transformed by the renewing of your mind, that ye may prove what is that good, and acceptable and perfect, will of God" (Romans 12:2).

One of the greatest struggles that I had as an adolescent was carrying out what I knew to be God's will in my every day life. I knew in my spirit what God wanted me to do, but it clashed in my mind, because my mind wanted to carry out the desires of my flesh. One of the spiritual truths that revolutionized my life was that the renewing of the mind is a prerequisite in order for one to do God's will.

I've read a lot of material concerning this topic, but I've found that most of it only emphasizes the psychological part of renewing the mind. It seems that there's a certain fear of speaking about the spiritual forces that have control over the minds of many Christians. The purpose of this book is to awaken you to the reality of these spiritual forces in the Believer's conscience, which divine or demonic, can in one way or another affect the functioning of your mind.

"Do Not Be Conformed to this World"

Every born-again Christian desires change and transformation in their life. The problem is that the majority of them don't know how to do it. For years and years preachers and evangelists have talked to the people about having to change to be able to reach a greater level of holiness, but they never told them how to do it. I don't know if you've had the same experience as I have, that I've sat and heard preachers preach to me about holiness and exhort on holy living, but I go home feeling like they gave me a diagnosis, but they didn't provide me with the cure.

After salvation, the renewal of the mind is the second most important step in the life of any person. When you begin to get this revelation, you'll arrive to the conclusion that it is you that has to renew your mind, and that God won't do it for you. The first decision that a Believer should make is that he won't conform to this world any longer. This simply means that we no longer follow the pattern or ways of this world as a norm or style for our lives.

I've noticed that one of the major problems with many Believers that don't think spiritually is that they try to live a new life while keeping the ideas and philosophies of this world, which is controlled by Satan the god of this world. In the same way that a liquid takes on the form of the vessel it is poured into, the Believer takes on the form of the system or ideas it moves in. In order to change we must abhor and reject everything that we receive from our families, society, culture, and surroundings that is in contraposition or discord with the Word of God.

The Apostle Peter explains it this way:

"Forasmuch as ye know that ye were not redeemed with corruptible things, as silver and gold, from your vain conversation received by tradition from your fathers" (1 Peter 1:18).

In this quest for transformation we can't even be sentimental with our family ties. If there is a certain form or way in my family or culture that is not in line with God's Word, I will renounce it no matter the price.

Before we can enjoy and experience this transformation, we must first renew our minds with new forms and patterns of thinking that are in harmony with the will of God. Don't think I'm talking about positive thinking. I am talking about a renewal of the mind that only those that are born of the Spirit of God and that have been made new creations can experience. It is this rebirth along with the life of Jesus in us that enables us to say a resounding "NO" to the old way of doing things and begin to program our minds to be able to totally obey God, and thus do His will.

The Spirit of the Mind

"That ye put off concerning the former conversation the old man, which is corrupt according to the deceitful lusts; And be renewed in the spirit of your mind" (Ephesians 4:22-23).

One of the erroneous concepts that we've got to change is the one that says that we're only in a conflict between good and bad ideas. This is much more serious than that, for there is a spirit that controls your mind and it affects your thoughts, words and actions. The mind can be controlled by the spirit of the old man, which was in us before we became saved. It is true that our old man was crucified with Christ on the cross, but according to Paul, we see that the spirit of this old man continues to affect our minds in one way or another.

The spirit of the minds of individuals that give their lives to the LORD must be renewed, because it is part of the old way of living that we had before becoming children of God. It is true that a saved individual is a new creation, because the Bible says so:

"Therefore if any man be in Christ, he is a new creature: old things are passed away; behold, all things are become new" (2 Corinthians 5:17).

Another way of explaining this, is when a person is saved he receives a new spirit inside. That spirit is the spirit of the resurrected Christ. Though this is not the theme of this book, let us not scorn the importance of developing and training that spirit.

The mind can be compared to a computer that works according to its programming. For many years our culture, our family, the society we live in, and the circumstances surrounding us have programmed our minds. Paul told the Ephesians that before a person becomes saved, he is under the influence of the spirit of Satan (Ephesians 2:1-3). The major influence of that spirit is in the mind, because whoever controls the mind of a person also controls his will and his actions. I'm not trying to say that all of these people have a demon in their minds, but the spirit that has the major influence on them is the spirit of this world, which is the spirit of Satan and his demons.

What Is Renewal?

If you were able to understand the last chapter about the different states of mind in the sinner and the Believer, you will realize the great need that every Believer has to renew his mind so that he can do the will of God. There's a difference between an individual changing in his spirit and changing in his mind. When talking about the spirit of a sinner, a new birth is necessary. We receive a new spirit, which is *"the new man, which after God is created in righteousness and true holiness"* (Ephesians 4:24). This is not the same with the mind. We don't receive a new mind, but we stay with the same old mind, which must be renewed in order to be free from the old spirit, which is of the old man.

What does it mean to renew something? It means to restore it to its original state. We use the same object and we cleanse it from what is old and antiquated, so that it might look new again. The Bible is full of exhortations, which admonish us to forget about the old way of living, so that we can get on with the new way of living. Another word we can use for this is sanctification, which deals not so much with our salvation, but with the changing of our character after we've been born-again. One of the great errors among some Christian groups is comparing salvation and sanctification as being the same. Sanctification is very important if we are to please God and show a good testimony here on earth. We can distinguish these two as follows: salvation is instantaneous, but sanctification is progressive. That is why we present a saving Jesus to sinners, and a sanctifying Jesus to those that are already Believers.

Having said the latter we don't want to rob the importance of the sanctification of the Believer, from the moment he is saved. It is the will of God that people would begin to separate themselves from everything that is not of God's nature and character from the moment they are born again. Only Believers can be sanctified, because residing on the inside of them is the resurrection power of Jesus, which enables them to be holy.

Even though we have that resurrection life inside of us, the reality is that our minds have been programmed by the old life for so many years that now in order to truly obey the desires of the Lord, we have to transform our way of thinking.

After so many years with my mind programmed to think sin, sickness, poverty, and failure, could I possibly renew my mind to do the good, acceptable, and perfect will of God? In the following, we will study the methods that God has given us in order to renew our minds. Read and study them over and over again. Ask the Holy Spirit to help you and you will notice a change in the way you think and act.

1 - Renewal through the Blood

"How much more shall the blood of Christ, who through the eternal Spirit offered Himself without spot to God, cleanse your conscience from dead works to serve the living God?" (Hebrews 9:14).

It is impossible for anyone to experience mental peace, unless they are at peace with God and with themselves. The unsaved individual lives under a constant state of mental and emotional pressure, because he knows he is under guilt and condemnation (Roman 2:15). This guilt proceeds from the conscience of man, which God placed in him to accuse or defend his thoughts. It is safe to say that every sinner knows that he's pinned beneath the wrath of God, even if he doesn't want to openly admit it.

Sinners try many methods to silence this accusation, by doing good works, educating their minds or practicing religion. But, neither of these can solve their problems. The only way is through the blood that Jesus shed for them on the cross. The essence of our salvation is that no person could be saved except through faith in the sacrifice of Jesus. It's not enough to believe in Jesus, you have to believe in the power of His blood, for without the shedding of blood there is no forgiveness of sins (Hebrews 9:22).

This is what the Bible calls redemption. We were purchased and delivered from the legal right that Satan had to us. Redemption involves the forgiveness of all sins, receiving a new nature, and the expulsion of guilt and condemnation. This redemption affects our spirit, soul, and body.

How Could I Be Made Righteous?

We're made righteous or justified before God, as a result of this redemption. You can only experience this by faith, which enables us to enter into communion and right standing with God. Mental peace is also a result of justification. *"Therefore, having been justified by faith, we have peace with God through our Lord Jesus Christ"* (Romans 5:1). The peace is experienced in the mind of an individual, after being reconciled to God through the blood of His Son Jesus Christ. This reconciliation takes place in the mind, because before being saved we were enemies with God in our minds (Colossians 1:21).

How does this happen? The Bible states that there was a wonderful exchange that took place at the cross. 2 Corinthians 5:21 says, *"For He made Him who knew no sin to be sin for us, that we might become the righteousness of God in Him (Jesus Christ)."* Jesus carried all of our sin and guilt and now when we believe in His blood, all of His righteousness is transferred or credited unto us. If the sinner would just understand this, he would realize that receiving Christ is the best deal a person could ever make in his entire life.

Discovering this truth is what radically transformed my Christian life. Though I've been a Christian since my childhood, my mind was filled with guilt and condemnation from the things I had done and the things I hadn't done. It is sad to say that today multitudes of Believers live enslaved to their past, because they haven't understood that the blood of Jesus has erased their past completely and that heaven no longer has any record of that past.

The Blood Gives You the Victory

The reason that so many sincere Believers struggle to win the battle in their minds is that they don't know that the blood saves them, gives them acceptance in heaven, cleanses them from all sin, makes them friends of God, and that it gives them legal authority over sin, demons, and sickness.

Thank God for the blood that cleanses our conscience from all dead works! A conscience that has been cleansed by the blood will produce a mind that is free from guilt and condemnation, which will be able to stand against the devil when he tries to bring thoughts of the past or of what could have been. We know that this fight never ends, because the enemy keeps attacking us even after we've repented of our sins.

The difference is that we that know the power of the blood of Jesus know how to make the accuser of the brethren flee from us. When he accuses me of something that is from the past and under the blood I say, *"It is true that I sinned, yes I did it, but I also repented and Jesus cleansed me with His blood, so what are you going to do now?"*

If you want to make the devil run from you at the speed of light, do what I do to him.

2 - Renewal through the Holy Ghost

The Holy Spirit is the creative force of God, and because of that, He has the power to produce a change in the minds of individuals that have put their faith in Jesus. Every bit of renewal in the life of a Believer depends on how much he yields to the operation of the Holy Spirit in his life. The Bible speaks of a renewal in the spirit of our minds. It takes more than philosophy or doctrine to renew the mind of an individual, because like we said before, the mind either is a slave to the spirit of Satan or to the Spirit of God. So, it takes a Spirit to deal with spiritual things. It is the Holy Spirit that makes the power of the blood of Jesus real. Every revelation that we can receive concerning who we are and the things we can do through Christ will come through total dependency on the Holy Spirit.

The Holy Spirit always works in harmony with our spirit. We've already said that salvation first takes place in the spirit, but that isn't God's total plan. After being saved through the blood and the Holy Spirit, God wants us to move in the rest of our being so that we can walk in complete sanctification.

God desires to reveal everything that He has provided for our total victory to us. There are things we don't even know exist, but God has them in store for those who love Him. The Bible guarantees us that,

> *"Eye has not seen, nor ear heard, nor have entered into the heart of man, the things which God has prepared for those who love Him"* (1 Corinthians 2:9).

The Holy Spirit first reveals these things to our spirits and then to our minds.

Ask the Holy Spirit to Help You

We desperately need the help of the Holy Spirit in order to renew our minds. But, before we can do this we need to know the Holy Spirit for who He really is. He is not just energy or a cosmic force as some have described Him. The Holy Spirit is God, and we should revere and serve Him as God. Everything that God does on the earth is done through the work of the Holy Spirit. Not only is He God, but He is also a person with a mind, emotions and a will. Therefore, you can have a relationship and communion with Him. Don't be afraid or feel silly to speak to Him and ask Him to help you renew your mind and reveal new thoughts and truths to your mind.

Don't even think for a moment that just reading the Bible is enough to transform your mind. It is the truth that the Holy Spirit reveals, that will transform your mind from the old way of thinking to God's way of thinking. Jesus said in reference to the Holy Spirit,

"However, when He, the Spirit of truth, has come, He will guide you into all truth; for He will not speak on His own authority, but whatever He hears He will speak; and He will tell you things to come" (John 16:13 NKJV).

He can do it because He searches the deep things of the mind of God and He shares them with the children of God, which are formed in His image.

This is how the Holy Spirit works to renew our minds. According to the Apostle Paul, it is the spirit of man that knows the things in that man. There are memories, which are hidden in us that affect our way of thinking, talking and living. If you totally yield to the Holy Spirit, He will do three things:

1) Strengthen your spirit,
2) Reveal the areas of your mind that need renewal,
3) Bring renewal to your mind through the Word.

3 - Renewal Through the Word

"For the Word of God is living and powerful, and sharper than any two-edged sword, piercing even to the division of soul and spirit, and of joints and marrow, and is a discerner of the thoughts and intents of the heart" (Hebrews 4:12 NKJV).

The Word of God is what the Holy Spirit uses in order to renew the mind of the Believer. As we stated before, the majority of the enemy's control is in the minds of people, because whoever controls your mind controls your whole life. We are in a battle of ideas, the ideas of God versus the ideas of God's archenemy Satan. The renovation of the mind is nothing more than being brainwashed with the Word. You wash your mind from Satan's ideas and you replace them with God's ideas.

The Word of God is the sword of the Spirit. That is why the Word has the ability to cut out all of the thoughts that we had in the old man. The Word penetrates to the deepest parts of the soul and mind and it brings the secret thoughts into the light. The Word is light, and it shines on the most hidden parts of your soul and it drives away all of the darkness, which is a result of the old, sinful, and wicked way of living.

Every time that the Bible talks about renewal, purification, or the salvation of the soul, it is referring to the renewal of the mind. All of these make up the process of sanctification; the mind is saved (rescued) from the power of sin, cleansed from the guilt of sin, and renewed from the presence of sin.

We must realize that we must make the decision if we want our minds to be renewed by the Word of God. It takes an attitude of meekness and humility to accept that our way of thinking has been wrong and we must be willing to cut out everything that is not in agreement with the Word of God from our minds. James shows us how to do it:

> *"Therefore lay aside all filthiness and overflow of wickedness, and receive with meekness the implanted word, which is able to save your souls"* (James 1:21 NKJV).

The Word has the power to save our souls, but we

have to decide to do two very important things in order for this to take place:

1) A decision to separate ourselves from sin
2) Receive the Word with meekness and humility without questioning.

How does this become practical? It functions just like the law of physics that says two objects cannot occupy the same space at the same time. Two ideas cannot simultaneously occupy your mind. That's why emptying your mind and leaving it blank like some (Eastern religions) suggest is not the answer. We have to fill our minds with the Word of God, so that we won't have room for everything else that isn't of God. Where there was hate, now there is love, where there was fear, there is confidence, where there was doubt, there is faith, and where there was sin, there is now righteousness.

Meditating on the Word

The art of meditating is an awesome help in renewing your mind with the Word of God. I'm not talking about transcendental meditation where we empty our minds or fix them on something sensational or fantasy. Meditating on the Word is simply taking a portion of Scripture and thinking on it for a period of time until you perceive that the Word has not only penetrated your mind, but your heart as well.

Many of the dilemmas that Christians face are because they think on negative things so much that they get to a point of desperation, worry and anxiety. Everybody practices meditation in one-way or another. The question is what are you meditating on? When you go to bed at night and begin to reflect on the events of your day, you are meditating. What would you do if the doctor told you that you had an incurable disease? You would meditate or ponder the possibility of dying prematurely.

God, who knows the power of your mind, is the one who through His Word, advises us to meditate on His Word, so that there can be a change in our way of thinking and acting. Not only will meditation change your way of thinking, but it will also help you realize the success that you so desire. God told Joshua:

> *"This Book of the Law shall not depart from your mouth, but you shall meditate in it day and night, that you may observe to do according to all that is written in it. For then you will make your way prosperous, and then you will have good success"* (Joshua 1:8 NKJV).

4 - Renewal by the Confession of Your Mouth

> *"Who satisfies your mouth with good things, So that your youth is renewed like the eagle's"* (Psalm 103:5 NKJV).

We have to do more than just read the Word in order for the Word of God to be more effective in the renewing of our minds. God's goodness and blessings come with His Word. The confession of your mouth is a marvelous and powerful tool that can radically change a person's life. The words that you speak can be a great blessing to your life or they can become a curse to you and affect your mental peace, health, the state of your family, your financial situation, your spiritual and physical progress, and the length of your life.

The Bible supports what I just said. We see an example in Proverbs 18:21 (NKJV), *"Death and life are in the power of the tongue, and those who love it will eat its fruit."* Every thought that you think needs to come out of your mouth in order to materialize. It is the things that you imagine and then speak that eventually become reality. Everything that is in the spiritual realm can be transferred into the physical realm through your confession and the words that you speak.

James says in his epistle,

"And the tongue is a fire, a world of iniquity. The tongue is so set among our members that it defiles the whole body, and sets on fire the course of nature; and is set on fire by hell" (James 3:6 NKJV).

If the tongue can defile the body, then it can heal and renew it as well. If it puts the power of creation into action, then we can say that it affects our minds, because it is the mind that gives it ideas to initiate the creating process. Your tongue can create a world of good or evil. We call this positive or negative confession.

Psalm 103:5 tells us that the Lord satisfies our mouth with good things for our renewing. God's Word should be continually in your mouth, so that you can continually be renewed. Refuse to confess any thought that is not in agreement with the Word of God, and confess all of those promises of spiritual, mental, emotional, physical, financial, and domestic peace that are in His Word. Negative thoughts will always pay your mind a visit, but you have the power to reject them through the confession of your mouth. *A thought that isn't spoken or written will eventually die of loneliness and boredom.*

Be like the eagle, which goes to a solitary place when it is tired or weary and finds a rock to rest on. The first thing it does is it gets rid of the old beak and with its new beak it cleans its feathers. It stays there until it grows new feathers. In other words, it renews itself. Abandon all negative confession about yourself, your family, and your circumstances and begin to speak with a new mouth filled with God's Word. Sooner or later your mind will have to adjust itself to the new way you are speaking and you'll be able to mount up to God's heights like a renewed eagle.

> *"But those who wait on the Lord shall renew their strength; They shall mount up like eagles, They shall run and not be weary, they shall walk and not faint"* (Isaiah 40:31).

5 - Renewal Through Praise

Wherever praise and worship is, there is renewal. We can tell if a church is walking in the renewal of the Holy Spirit by the way they praise God. Praise always changes our concept of God's character. A Believer who has discovered the power and blessing of praise will be in a continual state of renewal and transformation. When our minds are flooded with the presence of God, which comes as a result of praise, the way that we see God, our circumstances and ourselves will change.

Praise renews us, because we forget about ourselves and we totally concentrate on the love, holiness and power of God. Our entire being; spirit, soul and body seek communion with the Creator in an atmosphere of praise. When we begin to exalt the greatness of God we are putting our thoughts on Him. The result will always be peace, rest and security.

Praise lets your mind rest and it brings it into harmony with God. It is during times of praise and worship that our minds are filled with God's thoughts, which are higher, greater and more abundant than ours are. Let's allow the Word to tell us about the blessings that we receive when we surrender our minds to God through praise and worship.

> *"You will keep him in perfect peace, whose mind is stayed on You, because he trusts in You"* (Isaiah 26:3).

Chapter Four

Tearing Down Strongholds

"For though we walk in the flesh, we do not war according to the flesh. For the weapons of our warfare are not carnal but mighty in God for pulling down strongholds, casting down arguments and every high thing that exalts itself against the knowledge of God, bringing every thought into captivity to the obedience of Christ, and being ready to punish all disobedience when your obedience is fulfilled" (2 Corinthians 10:3-6 NKJV).

What we are about to deal with now is part of the renewal of the mind, however I thought it important enough to dedicate a whole chapter to this topic. We're going to get to the core of the title of this book. As I stated in the introduction, it was my observation of Believers trying to do spiritual warfare and beating the air instead of pulling down strongholds in their minds that inspired me to write this book. This has caused frustration for many Believers who try to do spiritual warfare and don't win, because they just beat the air.

It is so sad to know that many Christians are foreign to what I just said, because of their ignorance or by intent. This can be partly blamed on the modern mentality of trying to explain and solve people's problems through psychology and ignoring the place that the devil and his demon cohorts possess in the lifestyles and conduct of people. We have to understand that we live and move in two realms, the physical or natural and the spiritual or the supernatural. Even though we live in the physical realm we cannot fight according to the physical world, but we must fight according to the Spirit. The battle for our minds is not a physical battle; it is a spiritual one. This is why we must understand the reality of the spiritual strongholds that occupy room in the minds of so many Believers.

What Is a Stronghold?

In the Old Testament a stronghold was a high place, which was used during times of war for two purposes, 1) To watch out for the enemy and, 2) To serve as protection for the city against the enemy. They were fortresses built in strategic locations in order to effectively stand against and counter attack the enemy. When David fled from Saul he hid in a stronghold (1 Samuel 23:14-19). Can you see why in the Psalms, David refers to the Lord as his Stronghold or Fortress?

According to what I just said, not all strongholds are bad. There can be two kinds of fortresses in the minds of Believers; the fortresses that the Holy Spirit builds up through the Word of God, and the strongholds that the devil erects through his deceptions and lies. I must tell you that before we can allow God to build strongholds in our minds, we must first destroy the strongholds that the enemy has erected in our minds. Nobody can build a house in the same place where another house already stands. They have to tear down the old one in order to build up the new one. In the same way, the kingdom of God cannot be built in our minds until we've first destroyed the control and influence of the kingdom of darkness.

We're going to discuss the strongholds that the devil erects in our minds from the day that we are conceived in our mother's womb. Paul calls these strongholds *"imaginations and every high thing that exalts itself against the knowledge of God"* (2 Corinthians 10:5 NKJV). We can also call them thoughts that elevate themselves above the knowledge of God.

I would define a spiritual stronghold in the mind as a system of ideas or a train of thought, which controls our way of seeing things in one way or another, and is the pattern from which our conduct is derived. These trains of thought govern and control individuals, families, communities, nations, churches, and even denominations. These strongholds are what give Satan dominion and authority over so much of the human race.

Satan's Strongholds

We know without a doubt that the mind of an unsaved individual is a satanic stronghold, which controls everything they do or say. This is not a shock, because as we said before, the satanic nature is the inheritance of every human and cannot be rid of unless one becomes born-again. The individual that doesn't know the Lord and who isn't born-again can't do anything to tear down the stronghold that the enemy has erected in their mind or heart until he comes to Christ.

We are aware that people try to do all they can to improve themselves, but instead of these things helping them what they do is erect spiritual strongholds in their minds, which take them further away from God. This is the tragedy of trying to substitute Jesus with religion, humanism, positive thinking, philosophy, and other means of self-help. Beware of spiritual or mental self-improvement methods that don't involve the following: *being born-again, departing from sin, and depending on the Holy Spirit.*

We've already discussed the strongholds that are in the minds of unbelievers, but now we want to deal with the satanic strongholds that are in the mind of Believers. There is a battle going on, which we cannot ignore. Satan wants to keep us in slavery to his thoughts and ideas, so that we cannot become vessels of God, to destroy His works on the earth. Before we can come against these strongholds that the devil has erected in our mind, it is of the uttermost importance that we find out where they come from. Why am I the way that I am? Why do I think the way that I think? Why do I do the things I do? If you understand this well, not only will you be able to destroy those strongholds, but you will also be able to prevent Satan from establishing new ones in your life. Where do these strongholds come from?

1 - Inheritance from Your Parents

Have you ever heard someone excuse their behavior by saying that their parents or grandparents were that way? Two things that the Bible clearly teaches us are that a parent's blessing will come upon their children and that the parent's curses will also come upon their children. Psalm 103:17 establishes the former: *"But the mercy of the Lord is from everlasting to everlasting on those who fear Him, and His righteousness to children's children."* What about the curse? God said to Moses:

> *"And the Lord passed before him and proclaimed, 'The Lord, the Lord God, merciful and gracious, long-suffering, and abounding in goodness and truth, keeping mercy for thousands, forgiving iniquity and transgression and sin, by no means clearing the guilty, visiting the iniquity of the fathers upon the children and the children's children to the third and fourth generation"* (Exodus 34:6,7 NKJV).

We have inherited many of the negative attitudes and things that we have in our lives from our ancestors. This is even scientific fact. They call them "inherited illnesses." Every sin, rebellion, demon, and attitude that was in our ancestors wants to operate in our lives. We are heirs to the spiritual things of our parents just as we are of the physical things. Everybody knows that there are certain families where everyone lies, commits adultery, practices witchcraft, or gets divorced. With this said, I want to imply that there is a possibility that some of these strongholds in our minds were inherited.

We can eliminate these strongholds in two different ways. **The first way is to be born-again.** Through the redeeming of the blood of Jesus, Satan lost all legal right to our spirit, soul, and body. The Apostle Peter tells us in 1 Peter 1:18-19 (NKJV):

> *"Knowing that you were not redeemed with corruptible things, like silver or gold, from your aimless conduct received by tradition from your fathers, but with the precious blood of Christ, as of a lamb without blemish and without spot."*

Every Believer that knows this has already won half of the battle, because he knows how to put a permanent "STOP" to every sin and curse, which came through his ancestry. He knows that now he is a part of a new generation, the children of God.

The second way to destroy these strongholds is through an act of renouncing and receiving deliverance. If you understand the things that we just finished discussing, then you yourself can stand against everything that comes to your mind to contradict the Word and renounce it in the name of Jesus. When you know that you've been redeemed you can say to those sinful thoughts:

> *"You have no legal right to occupy my mind, because I've been redeemed from aimless conduct received by tradition from my ancestors by the blood of Jesus. I renounce your control in my life in the name of Jesus. There was pride through my family, but now in Christ there is humility, my ancestors were liars, but I know Christ who is the truth, hatred controlled my parents, but I am controlled by the love of God."*

2 - Our Society and Culture

Each one of us is a product of the society and culture of the cities and countries, which we were born and raised in. Our ways of thinking have been formed by all of the ideas we've received through our education, books that we have read and the values and behavior that are accepted in our culture and society.

It makes no difference if we love our countries; we have to admit that many of the concepts that are birthed in our nationality and culture are not inspired by God's Word. These concepts become strongholds in the mind of individuals. That's why it is so difficult to convince people of the need to change their way of thinking and patterning their lives.

Even many Christians put their social and cultural convictions above those, which come from the Word of God. Some even become outraged when we tell them to abandon certain national customs that oppose what the Word says. What a tragedy that some prefer to be American or whatever their nationality before being Christian! It should not be this way, because the Bible declares that though we live in this world, we are not of this world. We must renounce every hidden and shameful thing even if it separates us from our national traditions and customs.

The Bible clearly states that this world is under the power of the evil one. In other words, Satan's influence has penetrated the arts, music, literature, and the customs of every country. The Apostle Paul admonishes the Philippians concerning this matter saying,

> *"that you may become blameless and harmless, children of God without fault in the midst of a crooked and perverse generation, among whom you shine as lights in the world"* (Philippians 2:15 NKJV).

In order for you to have victory in the destruction of the strongholds in your mind, you must first accept this testimony of the Word of God, and be willing to rid your mind of all that has anything to do with this "crooked and perverse generation."

3 - Your Past Experiences

Every Believer must make the decision whether he will accept what the Word of God says about his life, or whether he will depend on his own experiences to guide him. Our experiences are valuable as long as we don't use them to substitute or take precedence over God's Word. Many of the strongholds that are in the minds of individuals are a result of their past experiences. If we're not cautious enough, those experiences can take the place of God's Word and hinder us from putting God's Word into practice.

So many people don't believe in divine healing, because a member of their family got sick, was prayed for and yet still died! Many reject speaking in tongues because of a bad experience. Some people won't even make new friends, because of bad experiences or betrayal of former friends. These are cases when past experiences become strongholds in the minds of these people and hinder them from enjoying the blessings of God.

The Word of God is the only absolute truth and it is eternal, contrary to the experiences of life, and is not subject to time or space. Don't ever think that a truth or principle from the Bible is not true just because it may not seem to have worked for you. If we do that we will be left without the only absolute truth in life, which is the eternal, infallible, and immutable Word of the Living God. Don't ever relinquish your faith because of your past experiences, but let you faith stand firm on the only real truth, the Word of God.

"Because all flesh is as grass, and all the glory of man as the flower of the grass. The grass withers, and its flower falls away, but the Word of the Lord endures forever" (1 Peter 1:24-25 NKJV).

4 - Religious Tradition

"He said to them, 'All too well you reject the commandment of God, that you may keep your tradition'" (Mark 7:9 NKJV).

I dare to say that more people will go to hell because of erroneous religious training, than people will from communism. There's not a more difficult stronghold to remove from a person, than the stronghold of religious tradition. There is something about religious ideas that people acquire that even by appearing to them Jesus Himself couldn't rid them of. It's fairly easy to renounce the things we've received from our ancestry and culture. However, when it comes to the things that certain individuals have received in their religious training, some would rather lose their soul before renouncing them.

I have encountered individuals who through the Bible I have convinced that they are wrong, but they end up saying to me, *"I know what you're telling me is the truth and according to the Bible, but I can't change because this is the way my church or parents taught me to be."* This is proof of an individual that has demonic a stronghold in their mind, which can not only take them to hell, but can also impede them from enjoying the best that Jesus has to offer.

That is why we have to be careful with many of the doctrines and teachings that we receive. It doesn't matter how charismatic or eloquent a teacher is. If any teaching leads us astray from fidelity to Jesus Christ and contradicts the Word of God we should reject it, so that it won't become a stronghold in our minds. Every Believer should go directly to the Word himself, when he perceives some teaching or doctrine that isn't in harmony with what God's Word clearly says.

I'd like to share a couple of sentences from the book *The Three Battlegrounds*, by Francis Frangipane, which relate to what I'm saying:

> *"Even true teachers can innocently communicate false doctrines. It does not matter how sincere our Bible teacher is. If what we are being taught does not lead us into Christ's love, His holiness or His power; if we are not being prepared in these spiritual dimensions for Jesus and, through Him, for others, that doctrine is a stronghold which is limiting and oppressing us."*

Why Do Christians Commit Sin?

This question has been an enigma for Believers throughout the past 2000 years. How could it be, that after receiving the awesome life of Jesus in our hearts, we could still be inclined to commit sin? We can attribute part of the answer to the strongholds that Satan erects in the minds of Christians. No sincere Believer desires to sin, because he knows that sin is outright rebellion against God.

We can say that sin is the conclusive outcome of the spiritual strongholds that we mentioned beforehand. When Satan builds a stronghold in an individual's mind, that stronghold becomes the place from which he operates his authority. This explains why certain individuals are more inclined towards committing certain sins; one has problems with lying, another with being cunning, and others with adultery or sexual sins. It all depends on the nature of the stronghold that is in that particular individual.

If we don't get this, we will always be up and down spiritually, sinning today then repenting tomorrow and saying, "I'll never do it again," but the following day ending up back in the same boat. Some live this way, and then eventually decide to sell out to sin, since they can't have victory over it. The Bible declares to us, *"But each one is tempted when he is drawn away by his own desires and enticed"* (James 1:14 NKJV). This leads us to understand that within every individual lie desires, which he can be led astray by.

These strongholds serve as hiding places for sin in the minds of individuals. It isn't enough to ask for forgiveness of the sins you've committed. You must first deal with stronghold and the place where it manifests. It is possible to be a Christian and have what I call "Strongholds of Sin" in your mind. In actuality, when the Bible refers to the works of the flesh, it means nothing more than the strongholds of sin, which are in the mind and control the body to make us sin against God. Even though the flesh does the work, the flesh receives its orders from the mind.

Can you see why we have to renew and deliver our minds from every diabolic, demonic and worldly influence? It is useless trying to discipline the flesh, if we don't deal with our minds, which give orders to our flesh. If we want to have victory over sin, we must be willing to despise and reject every old train of thought, which we received as heirs of the Adamic nature. Let's wage spiritual warfare against those strongholds, which are used by Satan to cause us to sin.

Could There Be Demons in Me?

I know that what I'm about to say is controversial within Christian circles, but I feel responsible to share what I know to be true concerning this subject. Some theologians and Bible scholars say that it is impossible for a demon to enter into a Christian, because he is the temple of the Holy Spirit. This argument is more complicated than it seems on the surface. We know that man is a triune being, spirit, soul and body and that salvation begins in the spirit of man, not in the mind or physical. There is no way that a demon can possess (the spirit of) a Believer, which is born-again and who hasn't intentionally rejected Jesus.

The Bible warns Believers to guard their spiritual lives, so that Satan and his demons won't influence them. Paul says the following: *"Be angry, and do not sin, do not let the sun go down on your wrath, nor give place to the devil"* (Ephesians 4:26-27), and *"lest Satan should take advantage of us; for we are not ignorant of his devices"* (2 Corinthians 2:11). These two passages help us understand the possibility of giving place to Satan in our lives. Where? You ask. It can be in the soul (mind) or in the body.

After ministering deliverance to people for over 25 years, I've realized that most individuals who are oppressed by demon spirits have given the devil a legal right by allowing him to erect strongholds in their minds. I'm not saying that all strongholds are demons, but they can become the platform from which they take control of the other areas of the person's life.

It isn't God's plan for us to go from deliverance to deliverance or from transformation to transformation. Every Believer is responsible for dealing with the areas of their lives, which attract demons and sin, and should make a definite decision to be free from every demonic stronghold. Naturally, this is a process. In the meanwhile, if deliverance is necessary, then so be it. The goal is to have the character of Jesus Christ formed within us, so that we don't need any more deliverance, and that we can be vessels to deliver others that are in the beginning of this process.

Tearing Down the High Places

This is the most exciting part of this chapter. How do I tear down the strongholds, which hinder me from thinking God's thoughts and lead me to disobey His will? Start arming yourself with this thought of victory, *"I can destroy these strongholds in my mind, because God said so in His Word."* Don't make any more excuses and don't deny the existence of those strongholds. Thousands of people are never free in this area, because they live in denial. The first step for any kind of deliverance is to accept or acknowledge your bondage.

Realize that this is not an emotional or physical battle, but a spiritual one. Don't look at things the way they appear (2 Corinthians 10:7), but look at them through the reality of the Word and the Spirit of God. Immerse yourself in the Word and ask the Holy Spirit to expose every thought that exalts itself against the knowledge of God in your life. Remember what the great reformer Martin Luther said: *"Imagination is the devil's horse."* Every thought that opposes God, or that even causes the slightest doubt in His Word, is a thought or idea of the devil.

Do you want Satan to keep riding you horseback?

This means that you may have to change some reading and training habits. Without a serious decision to quit reading certain books, watching certain movies and listening to certain people, you will not be able to tear down those thoughts or imaginations, which oppose the knowledge of God.

The key to all of this is bringing every thought captive to the obedience of Christ. What does that mean? You are going to examine every thought that comes to your mind, and you will compare it to what God's Word says. If it is in complete harmony with the Bible and God's plan for you, you can accept it as part of your thinking. If a thought is contrary to God, it strays you from the knowledge of Him; it strays you from loving Jesus and from prayer, it tells you that a little sin won't hurt and that you don't have to go to church to be a Christian, or stops you from worshiping Jesus; it is a stronghold that must be torn down immediately.

The Weapons of Our Warfare

Since God knew that you wouldn't make it in your own strength, He has given you spiritual weapons with which you can go up to destroy those high places in your mind. What are the weapons of our warfare, which Paul refers to? Through the *Blood of Jesus* we can prepare our minds to not feel inadequate in battle and know that we are well able to stand and defeat Satan in spiritual war. Knowing that we are righteous because of the blood gives us authority to cast Satan out, because now he can't disable us with guilt and condemnation.

Through the *Sword of the Word,* you cut out everything that exalts itself against the knowledge of God in your mind. The Word has the ability to penetrate deeply and divide asunder between the spirit and the soul. It knows how to cut out everything that hinders the life of Jesus Christ from being manifested from your spirit to the rest of your being. Through the Word you can remind the devil who you are in Christ, and the authority that you have in Christ.

The Name of Jesus was given to us to enter into spiritual combat and affirm the victory that Jesus had at the cross of Calvary, by making a public spectacle of Satan and his demon hordes. At the mention of His name, every knee must bow in three different worlds (Philippians 2:10). In the name of Jesus, command the devil to flee from you once and for all. Don't be afraid to yell it at the devil, because sometimes he plays deaf so you have to make it clear that you mean business. Don't worry about looking ridiculous. All that matters is this; you win!

After you've done this, it is time to bless and *Praise the Lord. Praise* is a very effective weapon, because it causes you to take the focus off of your situation and concentrate on the Lord Jesus Christ. *Praise* always makes the devil flee, because he can't stand it when Jesus is given the glory that he desires for himself.

All of these are by faith and you must do them independently from your feelings. Protect yourself with the *Shield of Faith* as you fight. Declare your victory by faith and don't expose your mind or self to the strongholds of the enemy any longer. There is no better time than now, to build a stronghold of God in your mind through the Word and the Holy Spirit.

Strongholds That Occupy the Minds of Christians

1 - Pride
2 - Rebellion
3 - Doubt & Unbelief
4 - Fear
5 - Worry
6 - Resentment
7 - Complexes
8 - Religiosity
9 - Tradition
10 - Works of the Flesh

> *"I have pursued my enemies and overtaken them; neither did I turn back till they were destroyed. I have wounded them, so that they could not rise; they have fallen under my feet. For you have armed me with strength for battle; you have subdued under me those who rose up against me"* (Psalm 18:37-39).

Chapter Five

The Power of Thinking

"Now to Him who is able to do exceedingly abundantly above all that we ask or think, according to the power that works in us" (Ephesians 3:20 NKJV).

One of the least understood things is the role that the mind has in the formation and conduct of an individual. Our minds have more control over us than we are often ready to admit. This is often more so within Christian circles, because we sometimes focus so much on our spirit that we forget about dealing with our minds. Some Christian authors don't get into this subject out of fear of being misunderstood or labeled supporters of New Age philosophy or positive thinking.

Even though it bothers, it is sad to say that secular writers know more about the human mind than many Christian authors do. In reading the writings of several secular authors, I've noticed that the concepts that they have are a poor imitation of the concepts of God's Word.

That's why I'm not afraid to explore this dimension of us human beings, from a Biblical viewpoint.

The biggest problem with "positive thinking" authors is that they ignore the fundamental truth of the need to be born-again in order to permanently change in all three areas of life; spirit, soul and body. It is a dangerous thing to think that we can reform our minds through humanistic discipline without first repenting of our sin, which is the main cause for the mental condition of mankind.

A Mind That Has No Limits

"So God created man in His own image; in the image of God He created him; male and female He created them" (Genesis 1:27 NKJV).

It is an interesting thing to think about the first man that God created. The men we see walking the earth today is absolutely nothing like the man that God created in the Garden of Eden. The Scriptures say that God created man in His image. It is the image of God in man, which elevates him to a position of authority and unlimited intelligence. When God breathed His breath into man, He shared His divinity, glory, power, character, wisdom and intelligence. I'm not saying that this makes man equal to God, but it does make him similar to God in nature.

This is what caused the devil to be filled with envy, when he saw that God had created a new being that wasn't an angel and which He could have communion with him. The second chapter of Genesis gives us a clear picture of the authority and wisdom that Adam possessed. Adam was given the responsibility of naming all of the animals that God had created. Genesis 2:20 declares: *"So Adam gave names to all cattle, to the birds of the air, and to every beast of the field."* Can you imagine the mental capacity of that first man, who was able to give a name to every living creature? This shows us that Adam's mind was functioning to the full capacity that God enabled it to.

Scientists say that the most intelligent man that has ever lived didn't even use 15% of his mind. Why could this be? The fall of man hindered humanity from functioning at the mental capacity that it has the potential to function at. Born-again Christians are supposed to develop their mental capacity, because they have the image of God at their disposal. There is a dimension of the mind of Christ in the Believer where there are no limits and everything becomes possible, when our minds are connected to the Master Mind of the universe, the mind of Jehovah God.

A Mind Submitted to Your Spirit

This book is more for Believers in the Lord Jesus Christ and people that the Bible calls Born-again. In order to fully exploit the power of our minds we've got to have our minds totally submitted to our spirit. We can't allow our mind to exalt itself above our born-again spirit. If we did that we would become mental Christians, instead of spiritual ones.

A mind submitted to the renewed spirit of a man will begin to receive an influx of the awesome resurrection life, which resides in a saved individual. We're not suppressing the mind; we're talking about putting it in the place where God originally intended it to be. Believers shouldn't be led by their renewed minds, but the witness that the Holy Spirit ministers to our minds should lead us. There are many things of the Spirit that our minds won't understand until our spirit teaches it to our mind.

It was the image of God in Adam that gave him such a powerful mind. The image of God is not in our mind, but in our spirit. But, our minds and bodies will be impacted by the image of God in the measure that we submit them to our spirit.

How Does the Mind Affect the Body?

Our minds control our bodies more than we want to admit. When we hear the term "psychosomatic diseases" we have a tendency to mock the possibility of someone's thinking being able to affect their physical state. Reality is that many people get sick and even die prematurely, because they think they're sick or going to die young.

We can't deny that our emotional status affects our physical state. In the same way, our mental state can affect our bodies. I'm not trying to deny the fact that all disease and infirmity has a diabolic origin. If Satan can't make us sick because of our sin, it is possible that he will try to use our minds and emotions to afflict our bodies with sickness.

In essence man is an integral being, although we divide him into three parts for the sake of study. Whatever takes place in the spirit of a man, also affects his mind and body. What you think in your mind can affect your spirit and body. The state of your body can limit your spirit and your mind to a certain extent as well. No wonder the Bible tells us to love God with these three parts of us and to sanctify them. Paul said:

> *"Now may the God of peace Himself sanctify you completely; and may your whole spirit, soul, and body be preserved blameless at the coming of our Lord Jesus Christ"* (1 Thessalonians 5:23 NKJV).

The Power of Thinking

Thoughts Are Images

Thoughts are not merely ideas or concepts. They are pictured images, which define an idea or concept. We all think in images, because in order for the mind to remember or memorize it must first take a picture of whatever it is storing away. Anytime someone mentions something to you, you immediately picture an image of it in your mind. This is so true that when someone introduces something new to you, you always compare it with another image, which you already know and have an understanding of.

Another word for thinking is imagining. This means to make images in your mind. When someone says the word "car" we don't think about a flying mechanism, but we think about something that we see on the streets and highways of our cities. If we hear the word "dog" we don't think about the letters d, o, and g. We think about an animal that has four legs and barks. We don't think about a cat or a horse.

Every word that exists has an image, which defines its own characteristics and traits. Even words that define certain attitudes and virtues bring images to our minds when we hear them. It's not the same to hear the word "love" as it is to hear the word "hate." We immediately relate each to an activity or behavior that describes them.

This is why, the words that you store in your mind become the plan for your life, because they are living images that you have experienced or seen. It is these images, which determine the image that an individual has of the rest of the world and himself.

A perfect example of this is something that I experienced after leaving a glorious Church meeting, where the power of God was manifested. During a ministry trip to Central America, I was invited to eat with the host pastor of the church I ministered at. As we entered the restaurant, three boys came begging us to let them eat whatever remained on our plates after we were done eating. When we left the restaurant there were the three boys waiting for us to give them what they had asked. After we gave them some food, I thought about how the self-image of those boys was destroyed and how hard it would be for them to have it changed. Their image of life is for someone to do everything for them. It isn't an image of self-improvement and vision for a better future.

This should let you know that *The Battle for Your Mind* is not only a battle of ideas and concepts, but it is also a battle with the images that have been branded into our minds since childhood. Before we can change we have to erase those old and negative thoughts from our minds, so that we can paint new and positive images.

You Are What You Think

What we think eventually determines what we are. The Bible isn't wrong when it says, *"As he thinketh in his heart, so is he"* (Proverbs 23:7). If a thought remains in our minds long enough, it will become part of what we are in our hearts.

Oh, the great responsibility that we parents have in forming the character and personality of our children! By experience we know that the images we have in our minds were greatly influenced by our parents and teachers early in our childhood. If someone told us that we would amount to nothing in life, then they painted an image of inferiority, lack of ability and failure in us. My wife and I had to fight to erase the words that a teacher spoke to one of our sons, "You are dumb and you'll never be able to learn like your big sister."

I know by firsthand experience how important this is. Before I could be healed of my speech impediment, I had to change my self-image. There will always be individuals that will remind you of what you used to be and if you're not strong you will end up being that same person again. You're not what people say anyway, you are what God says you are. If you are saved you have a new image and that should determine the way you think.

If God says that I am righteous, then I am righteous. If God says that I'm His son, than that's what I am. If God says that I'm healed it doesn't matter how I feel, I am healed. If God says that I can prosper, then I can prosper. Allow me to give you my translation of 2 Corinthians 5:17: *"If any person is in Christ, he is a new creation, the old images are past and all things are made new."*

Memory and Imagination

Hear are some passages from my book *The Road to Success* (*La Escalera del fxito*), which will help you to understand the difference between memory and imagination:

> *"Someone once said that there are two kinds of thinkers in the world, those that think on their memories and those that think using their imaginations. The former are those that live in the past, pondering what could've been, and the latter are those that are constantly using their imagination to plan for the future.*

Dear reader, I'd like to ask you a question that will define which of the two you are. Where are you living, in your memory or in your imagination? If you're living in your memory, then you're living in the past, but if you live in your imagination, then you're launching yourself towards a future full of hope.

Don't think that it's always wrong to remember things from the past. Your memory should serve to think and meditate on the successes and victories of your past and how you obtained them. It should be a means for inspiration. This way your memory can become a great help and blessing to your life."

If you're born-again, then God wants you to learn to put those negative, sinful and rebellious thoughts of the past behind you. The tragedy with so many sincere Christians is that they insist on living off of the memories of what could've been and not on what was. As long as we cling to the past we will never be able to move ahead towards the future.

The Bible motivates us to forget about the memories that tie us to our past. The Apostle Paul had to deal with this area of his life and said,

"Not that I have already attained, or am already perfected; but I press on, that I may lay hold of that for which Christ Jesus has also laid hold of me. Brethren, I do not count myself to have apprehended; but one thing I do, forgetting those things which are behind and reaching forward to those things which are ahead" (Philippians 3:12-13 NKJV).

This verse leads us to believe that memories can hold us back and hinder us from going forward in God, but our imagination can thrust us forward towards our future, so that we can enjoy God's best for our lives.

God Works With Your Thoughts

There is a powerful verse that became life to me one day. Ephesians 3:20 says, *"Now to Him who is able to do exceedingly abundantly above all that we ask or think, according to the power that works in us."* The word "think" can also be translated imagine or visualize. As we stated before, the human mind has great power to imagine and visualize things. According to this verse, the outcome of our prayers doesn't solely depend on God, but also on our ability to envision or imagine what we're asking clearly.

God works with our thoughts. The reason we don't receive sometimes is because we don't have a clear-cut vision of what we're asking for. We can't expect healing with an image of sickness. We can't expect prosperity with an image of poverty and misery. I suggest that before you ask God for something, that you go and get a vision and an image from His Word concerning that thing.

I hope that you now realize the importance of your thoughts and how they determine the actual state of your life. There is great power stored up in that head you and I carry around, and it can make the difference between success and failure in your spiritual and natural life.

> *"The potential and possibility to help and bless humanity, which lies within the minds of mankind is just as undiscovered as the depths and abyss of the seas."*

Chapter Six

Thinking God's Thoughts

"The Lord knows the thoughts of man, that they are futile" (Psalm 94:11 NKJV).

"For My thoughts are not you thoughts, nor are your ways My ways, says the Lord. For as the heavens are higher than the earth, so are My ways higher than your ways, and My thoughts than your thoughts" (Isaiah 55:8-9 NKJV).

In the previous chapter we discovered how powerful the thoughts of man are and what they are able to accomplish. However, God's opinion of man's thoughts is that they are futile. When we compare God's infinite mind to ours, we have to concede to His opinion. Just think; if a mind without God can accomplish what humanity has accomplished until now, what could we discover or invent by uniting our minds with the power of God's mind?

God is not a mind like some false religions suggest, but He does have a mind. According to Genesis chapter 1, our minds were made in the image and likeness of His. God's will is that when we get born-again we can connect our minds to His mind, and that we can operate at the stature and level of this new position as sons of God.

I pray to God that this chapter will be a great inspiration to your life, and that it will help you to destroy the barriers that hinder you from receiving God's maximum blessing. Let's find out where you're at in your thinking first. I believe that no one can think the thoughts of God until they deal with, and have control over their own thoughts first. How is your thinking?

Do You Think Good or Bad?

> *"Finally, brethren, whatever things are true, whatever things are noble, whatever things are just, whatever things are pure, whatever things are lovely, whatever things are of good report, if there be any virtue and if there be any praise think on these things"* (Philippians 4:8).

Before Paul wrote the best spiritual recipe for mental peace, he indirectly gives us certain characteristics of the person, which has taken control of his thoughts. A positive mind that is filled with the Word always rejoices, is gentle with everyone, is never anxious for anything and makes its needs known unto God through prayer. This individual will experience a tremendous peace that surpasses human understanding. We know by experience that an individual that hasn't controlled his mind cannot experience such peace.

We know that it is only through the Word Of God and the Holy Spirit that we can control the mind, but it is we that make the decision to do it. The key is doing what God has said in His Word. Let's discipline our minds to only think things that bring peace and mental serenity to us. The last verse that we read tells us what to think about, every true, noble, just, lovely, good, virtuous and praiseworthy thing. If any thought is contrary to these things, then we shouldn't think it.

How do we attain this? Certainly not by trying to stop thinking negative and sinful things, the emphasis isn't the negative. The secret to taking control of your mind is to fill it with thoughts from God's Word, so much that there's no more room for Satan's thoughts to directly or indirectly occupy our minds. This is part of bringing every thought captive to the obedience of Christ.

It is worth doing this, because we will reap tremendous results, which will help us spiritually and naturally. The Bible promises that, *"the peace of God, which surpasses all understanding will guard your hearts and minds through Christ Jesus"* (Philippians 4:7 NKJV). This comes in agreement with Isaiah 26:3, *"You will keep him in perfect peace, whose mind is stayed on You, because he trusts in You."* If you learn to think right, then you won't need the help of a psychiatrist or you won't have to visit a cardiologist. Why? The peace of God is a result of a mind that thinks God's thoughts.

Rejecting Your Own Thoughts

An individual won't be able to draw near to God and receive His thoughts until he humbles himself and recognizes that God's littlest thought is bigger than his biggest thought. Sin has created such pride in people that they think that they are just as wise, if not wiser than God. We've even seen this attitude in many Christians that think they have a "better idea" about something, even though it contradicts the Word of God. This attitude has stopped many Believers from walking in God's perfect will. In the Bible, Paul gives us the solution for this:

"Let no one deceive himself. If anyone among you seems to be wise in this age, let him become a fool that he may become wise. For the wisdom of this world is foolishness with God. For it is written, He catches the wise in their own craftiness" (1 Corinthians 3:18-19).

I've observed how often the affluent of society come to Church to be saved, but they think that because of the wisdom, and accolades that they've attained in the world, that they don't have to go through the same process as every other normal or even more ignorant person has to go through. Paul's words are very clear concerning this. Nobody can attain the wisdom of God, unless they get rid of their own first. This isn't easy, because of the pride and inflated egos that we often have. It is a bit difficult for a mind that is wise according to the world's standards to agree with this other passage that Paul writes, *"but God has chosen the foolish things of this world to put to shame the wise"*.(1 Corinthians 1:27 NKJV).

Paul knew what he was talking about, because he had to make the same decision for his own life. Theologically speaking, Paul was a very intelligent and wise man in his time. However, it didn't take long before he realized that he'd have to put it all to the side in exchange for the mind of Christ if he wanted a true revelation of God. It couldn't have been easy for him to put those things aside, because according to him they were gain (Philippians 3:7). Had he not done it, then God wouldn't have revealed Himself to Paul in the awesome manner that He did. Are you willing to make the same decision? Repeat aloud with Paul and I,

> *"Yet indeed I also count all things loss for the excellence of the knowledge of Christ Jesus my Lord, for whom I have suffered the loss of all things, and count them as rubbish, that I may gain Christ"* (Philippians 3:8).

The Excellency of God's Thoughts

> *"Oh the depth of the riches both of the wisdom and knowledge of God! How unsearchable are His judgments and His ways past finding out! For who was known the mind of the Lord? Or who has become His counselor?"* (Roman 11:33-34 NKJV).

Omniscience is one of God's divine attributes. God knows everything! The human mind can't even begin to comprehend how immense and complex the mind of God is. In the previous verses we read two important questions. Who has known the mind of the Lord, and who has become His counselor? These two questions describe the problem with man trying to be God's counselor without understanding His mind. I've never felt competent enough to tell God what to do, how to do it and when to do it.

One of the reasons people don't receive the supernatural manifestation of God, is because they have the bad habit of trying to tell Him how to do it. If many times we can't even understand our own minds, how will we dare to try and understand God's and give Him orders? That is why God manifests Himself more in places where there isn't so much humanism present. Miracles happen when we allow God to be God and when we don't try to control Him. It is one thing to try to understand the mind of God and an entirely different thing to receive the mind of God. Even though we don't understand the mind of God, we can receive the blessings and benefits that come with receiving and manifesting His mind in our lives.

Maybe we won't understand the fullness of God's mind while we're here on earth, but we can understand enough of His mind concerning us to fulfill His will and purpose for our lives. Thank God for the Holy Spirit, who has been given to help us in this area. According to 1 Corinthians 2:10-11, it is the Holy Spirit that *searches all things, even the deep things of God, for no one can know the things of God except the Spirit of God.* The Holy Spirit is the third Person of the Trinity, which manifests the mind of God on the earth in this day. This is referred to as "Revelation." To reveal is to remove a veil that hides or covers something that is on the other side of that veil or curtain.

If we want to understand the mind of God we must seriously consider having communion with the only person that can reveal it to us. The Holy Spirit knows the mind of God for every situation of your life. There is nothing that He doesn't know. He knows about healing, demons, finances, family matters, professions, ministry, and the works of Jesus, etc.

All it Takes Is One Thought

One single thought can radically change your life forever. Why do I believe this? It has been one single idea or thought that has made people millionaires. That small idea became a product, which was bought by millions of people and it as a result the inventor or proprietor became a millionaire. If this is true with the human mind, then what can happen with an idea from the mind of God? We can't even imagine what a simple idea from God can produce in an individual, a family, a church, or a whole country. Satan knows this all too well. That is why he tries to get us to hold on to our own ideas and concepts, even though they don't work. How many ministries could explode in growth and in power if they'd be willing to receive an idea from God and carry it out?

One thought from God can make the difference between sickness and health, poverty and prosperity, a mediocre life and a life of success and a short life or a long one. I challenge you in the name of Jesus, to put your Mickey Mouse ideas aside and to seek God's ideas. Pay close attention to what the Bible says about God's thoughts, which can change your life and those who surround you.

> *"Many, O Lord my God, are Your wonderful works which you have done; and your thoughts toward us cannot be recounted to you in order; If I would declare and speak of them, they are more than can be numbered"* (Psalm 40:5 NKJV).

> *"O Lord, how great are Your works! Your thoughts are very deep"* (Psalm 92:5 NKJV).

"How precious also are Your thoughts to me, O God! How great is the sum of them!" (Psalm 139:17 NKJV).

How to Understand God's Ways?

God's ways are intimately related to His thoughts. An individual always acts according to his thoughts. If you know the way someone thinks, then you will know how he or she is going to act. You can't change someone's conduct unless you change the way they think. We can't act like God, until we know and think His thoughts. Therefore, if we know His thoughts, we'll know how He's going to act.

The ways of God are a mystery to many people, because they've never discovered or uncovered His thoughts. God doesn't only want to reveal His ways to us, but He wants to make His ways become our ways. But, this won't happen until His thoughts become our thoughts. The first step towards this is being born-again. Every born-again individual has the potential to realize the mind of Christ, but he has to continually receive the Word in order for him to think like God does. Even though Jesus had the mind of God, the Bible tells us that He was in constant communion with the Father. In order to understand God's ways we must do three things: be born-again, fill ourselves with the Word of God and totally depend on the Holy Spirit.

We can't think for one minute that we can walk in the ways of the Lord while we have our own thoughts, the world's thoughts, or Satan's thoughts in our minds. *The Battle for Your Mind* will be won with the thoughts of God, not with our own. This is a spiritual battle, which involves spiritual thoughts. The only way to combat a diabolic thought is to fight it with a greater thought, the thoughts of God Almighty.

Receiving the Thoughts of God

Isaiah 55 gives us the process for receiving the mind of God.

1 - Thirst for the mind of God—Verse 1
2 - Know that it is by grace. It is free—Verse 1
4 - Establish our priorities— Verse 2
5 - Hear the Word of God attentively—Verse 3
6 - Seek God and call to Him in prayer—Verse 6
7 - Repent of our own thoughts and ways—Verse 7
8 - Receive His thoughts and ways through revelation of His Word—Verses 8-11

It is worth the effort to practice these things, because a wonderful change will occur immediately. Your life will be changed from a religious routine to an exciting life where every morning you wake up expecting God to do great things in you. Now you can walk in faith and expect miracles in your life. Your thoughts will no longer be toys in the hands of the devil to bring you doubt, weakness, and an identity crisis. The dynamic and awesome thoughts of God will bring fertility where there once was a dry and barren desert.

I'm not saying that *The Battle for Your Mind* is over. It will never end, but now you can enter into this battle thinking like the winner that you are. Is there even one of Satan's thoughts that can defeat God's? There is NO way! Arm yourself with health, healing, mental peace, prosperity, abundant life, anointing, power, and glory and you will discover that Satan's dominion has been broken off of your life forever. Now, you're really going to live like a true child of God; thinking the higher, precious, innumerable, deep, and powerful thoughts of Father God. *Glory be to God!*

Chapter Seven

A New Mentality

"For I know the thoughts that I think toward you, says the LORD, thoughts of peace and not of evil, to give you a future and a hope" (Jeremiah 29:11 NKJV).

God's thoughts are what enable us to have a new mentality. It is sad to say, but there are many new creations living with old mentalities. Like we said before, our minds have been programmed with so many ideas and concepts, which aren't God's. The first thing we should ask ourselves when a situation arises is: What does God say about this? The sad truth is that most people seek first the opinion of everyone else in the world before seeking God's. But, if we'd go to Him first, then we'd evade many problems.

The Bible is the only reliable source in which we can tap into all of God's thoughts concerning every problem, situation, and aspect of life. As I said before, God's thoughts are higher and greater than even the most intelligent person's thoughts. God even compares His thoughts to man's by saying: *"For My thoughts are not your thoughts, nor are your ways My ways"* (Isaiah 55:9 NKJV). What's the distance between Heaven and Earth? That's the same distance between our thoughts and God's thoughts. Now do you see how important it is for us to change our mentality?

If we desire to receive heavenly things and live at heaven's standard, then we must take our minds off of earthly things and expect to receive our thoughts from heaven. We don't have to go up to heaven to do this, because heaven already came to earth. The Bible tells us that the Word became flesh and dwelt among us, so that we could have a new mentality. If you've received the Living Word (Jesus Christ), and if you keep filling yourself with the written Word daily (the Bible), then your way of seeing things will change. You might change so much that your friends won't even recognize you anymore.

What Hinders Your Change of Mentality?

I just want to discuss one thing that hinders many Believers from acquiring the new mentality, which enables them to live as children of the King. Jesus had to deal with this obstacle in His own ministry. I am referring to tradition. Tradition can become a monstrous force that takes the place of God's Word and it can even make people think that it is God's Word. Tradition is based on the rules and commandments of men. There is slavery, regression and ignorance wherever tradition is. Tradition is nothing more than mankind's ideas of God, which became concrete in their minds.

In my pastoral experience, I've noticed that before I

can change the mentality of the people that come to my church, I must first destroy the traditional concepts and ideas, which religion, their culture, and the world system have imparted to them. It is amazing how loyal people are to their traditions, even when they know that they are no good. Some even defend their right to be sick or poor with such fervor! It is so incredible, yet so true that most preachers of the Word have to spend so much time destroying imaginations, which exalt themselves against the knowledge of God.

Sometimes when I preach at churches that are drowned in tradition, it takes me three or four days of teaching just to pull down the wrong concepts that the people have of God. It's funny how by the time I pull down those traditions and the people start to understand what I'm saying, it's already time for me to leave. In some instances it has been "hello and goodbye" because the moment I left, the people once again pick up with their traditions esteeming them as higher than the truth of God's Word. The world hasn't changed. Jesus told the religious folks of His day: *"All too well you reject the commandment of God, that you may keep your tradition"* (Mark 7:9 NKJV). In the name of Jesus, I prohibit you from putting this book down until you've finished this last chapter. You're about to read the best part of it.

1 - A Mentality of Righteousness

So many people live with a mentality of guilt and condemnation! It is essential for a Believer to get rid of the problem of guilt. A person with a guilty and condemnation mentality cannot be happy in their Christian life and they can never receive what God has for them. Guilt is a result of a sin consciousness. There is insecurity and weakness when there is a sin consciousness. Guilt also strips the Believer of his authority over Satan and hinders a Believer for believing God. A guilty person feels unworthy to fight the devil and too guilty to ask God for something.

The Word can set us free from guilt if we read and believe it. The Bible says that if you're saved, then you are no longer a sinner. Contrary to what religious tradition says, God says that now we are righteous. Paul affirms this over and over again in his epistles. Let's take a look at some examples.

> *"Therefore, having been justified by faith, we have peace with God through our Lord Jesus Christ"* (Romans 5:1).

> *"For He made Him who knew no sin to be sin for us, that we might become the righteousness of God in Him"* (2 Corinthians 5:21).

What we need to do is learn to deal with the accusations that Satan hurls at us concerning our past. It makes Satan's job easier if you have a guilt consciousness. A mind free from guilt knows how to stand toe to toe with Satan and shout:

> *"There is therefore now no condemnation to those who are in Christ Jesus, who do not walk according to the flesh, but according to the Spirit." "Who shall bring a charge against God's elect? It is God who justifies"* (Romans 8:1,32).

This is operating in the mind of Christ, because He had no guilt or condemnation in His mind.

A New Mentality

You can break that negative mentality of condemnation, because that which brought guilt and condemnation to you was destroyed by Jesus Christ at the cross of Calvary. The Son of God took all guilt and condemnation away and He empowered you to be free. You no longer live under the law of sin and death, *"For the law of the Spirit of life in Christ Jesus has made you free from the law of sin and death"* (Romans 8:2 NKJV). Allow your mind to bask in what that says and you'll be able to live a life with a righteous mentality.

2 - A Mentality of Power

The opposite of a mentality of power is a mentality of impotence, which is a result of guilt and condemnation. Guilt always produces spiritual weakness, because it makes an individual feel inferior in his relationship with God and in his stance versus Satan. You know when there is condemnation in your life. It seems as though there's been a leakage of energy and power in your mind and body. It benefits Satan to keep you under condemnation, because then you'll be powerless to destroy his works.

If your attitude towards the challenges of life is "I can't" then you haven't discovered that "I can do all things through Christ who strengthens me." The Bible says that God works according to the power that works in you. That is the same power, which raised Christ Jesus from the dead. Take a minute to imagine the power that resides in a Believer. This is not just a mental exercise and it isn't positive thinking, it is a reality that is clearly established in God's Word.

Your spiritual position is one of honor, power, and glory seated in the heavenly realms with Christ. This is what gives you power and authority over the power of darkness. What you and I need is the revelation of this reality, which we find in the first chapter of Ephesians. God wants you to know,

> *"what the exceeding greatness of His power toward us who believe, according to the working of His mighty power which He worked in Christ when He raised Him from the dead and seated Him at His right hand in the heavenly places far above all principality and power and might and dominion, and every name that is named, not only in this age but also in that which is to come"* (Ephesians 1:19-21).

This should be the mentality of every child of God that has been redeemed from the power of the devil by the blood of Jesus.

3 - A Mentality of Victory

Who said that we couldn't always live in victory? Who said that I couldn't be a successful person? Does the fact that I'm a Christian mean that I have to be at the tail of sinners and the world? Absolutely not! But, the traditional mind would answer these questions differently. If there is one thing that the Bible assures us it is that all of Christ's victory belongs to us.

A mentality a failure is demonic, because it takes away your vitality and prevents you from dreaming. If an individual doesn't know that his victory is already assured, then he's already a failure before he begins. Even if certain difficult things arise in my life, I'd rather always think that I'm going to succeed and have victory. I've been accused of being too victory minded, but the heroes of the Old Testament, Jesus, Paul, and every other great man in history was the same, so I'm in good company.

From Genesis to Revelation the Bible is full of promises for victory. It has been religious tradition that has said the contrary. It's a shame that the rules and traditions of men have voided these promises contained in the Word of God. But, glory to God that He is raising up a new generation of Believers around the world who are breaking these religious traditions and trains of thought and are daring to reclaim the victory, which is rightfully theirs. This is the generation that will crush the old serpent's head.

Here are some of those promises that will help you to change your mentality into a victorious one.

> *"Yet in all these we are more than conquerors through Him who loved us"* (Roman 8:37).

> *"But thanks be to God, who gives us the victory through our Lord Jesus Christ"* (1 Corinthians 15:57 NKJV).

> *"Now thanks be to God who always leads us in triumph in Christ, and though us diffuses the fragrance of His knowledge in every place"* (2 Corinthians 2:14 NKJV).

> *"For whatever is born of God overcomes the world. And this is the victory that has overcome the world— our faith"* (1 John 5:4 NKJV).

> *"He who overcomes shall inherit all things, and I will be his God and he shall be My son"* (Revelation 21:7 NKJV).

4 - A Mentality of Health

This may sound ridiculous, but there are people that only think about sickness and dying prematurely. Jesus didn't only die on the cross for our sins; He did it also for our infirmities. In a sense, most of humanity has a sickness mentality. From childhood we're taught to expect certain sicknesses during certain seasons. I'm not denying the reality of sickness, but I want to drive home a point.

The fear of death, which is part of the Adamic nature, is the main reason for this. However, this is different for Christians, through Jesus' sacrifice at the cross. God's Word says:

> *"In as much then as the children have partaken of flesh and blood, He Himself likewise shared in the same, that through death He might destroy him who had the power of death, that is, the devil, and release those who through fear of death were all their lifetime subject to bondage"* (Hebrews 2:14-15 NKJV).

If we understood this truth and the reality of what happened when Jesus died on the cross, then our attitude towards sickness would change. Sickness has no legal authority over the children of God. The redemption of Christ covers the sins as well as infirmities of mankind. The problem is that for years religion has ferociously opposed this truth. Sometimes I think that doctors want to see people healed more than most preachers do.

This has caused most of the Christian world to have a sickness mentality. How do I know when someone has a sickness mentality? The individual that has it holds fast to these three reasons for being sick: they think it is normal, they think it is God's will and they think that it perfects us as Christians. If we see the way that Jesus dealt with sickness, we'll notice that He kicked those excuses to the side. Wherever He went, He healed diseases and treated sickness just like He did demons. He never let someone remain sick to glorify God or be perfected.

Where did the Church get their doctrines on sickness? They got them when they lost the power of the Holy Spirit and began giving priority to the traditions of men rather than the Word of God. Don't forget what we said before about strongholds. These false teachings, which were accepted by the institutionalized church, became trains of thought that, dominate in today's churches and denominations.

Jesus said: *"And ye shall know the truth, and the truth shall make you free" (John 8:32).* The only thing that can make a person free from that mentality is the truth of the Word. I remember as a child and a teen that I would get sick at certain times of the year. One of these times was Holy Week. It seemed that every year during Holy Week, I'd be in bed with fever and the flu. It was so normal for me that I expected it. I had a sickness mentality. But, there was an immediate change in my life when I received the revelation of the power of the Word and the power of faith. It was the words that I'm sharing with you throughout this chapter that changed my life. Even though the devil's attacks always come, I face them differently: Nahum is the healed rejecting sickness and not the sick trying to get healed. Why? I've discovered God's thoughts concerning my right to be healed.

> *"And ye shall serve the Lord your God, and He shall bless thy bread and thy water; and I will take sickness away from the midst of thee"* (Exodus 23:25).

> *"But He was wounded for our transgressions, He was bruised for our iniquities: the chastisement of our peace*

was upon Him; and with His stripes we are healed" (Isaiah 53:5).

"Who forgiveth all thine iniquities, Who healeth all thy diseases" (Psalm 103:3).

"How God anointed Jesus of Nazareth with the Holy Ghost and with power, who went about doing good, and healing all that were oppressed of the devil; for God was with Him" (Acts 10:38).

"But if the Spirit of Him who raised Jesus from the dead dwells in you, He that raised Christ from the dead shall also quicken your mortal bodies by His Spirit that dwelleth in you" (Romans 8:11).

Now you decide which one has greater value; the infallible and eternal Word of God or the traditions of men. Allow the Holy Spirit to change your mentality from one of sickness to one of health and healing, so that you can be healed and be used to heal others.

5 - A Mentality of Abundance

Out of all of the things that conflicted with my mind, this was the toughest. That is why I'm not surprised when I hear people from my same background attacking every teaching that sounds like prosperity teaching. It seems that Satan has convinced even the most "spiritual and holy" Christians that it's all right for sinners to enjoy the blessings of this earth, but not the children of God, which are the rightful heirs of them all.

The poverty mentality has done more to hinder the advancement of the gospel than communism and humanism have. It is this mentality that has kept whole countries under spiritual and physical misery. A church with this mentality will never reach the world with evangelism the way God has commanded us to. We've been called to change the world and without money we won't do it. This might clash with religious thinking, but it's the truth.

Prosperity and abundance are divine laws, which work as long as our motives are correct and as long as we meet the conditions that God has established in His Word. We shouldn't be afraid to expect to receive those blessings that the Bible promises are ours. If everything belongs to God and we are His legal heirs (Romans 8:17), then we should enjoy some of that inheritance here on earth without reserve. God wants to give us financial abundance for three reasons: first, to extend His kingdom throughout the earth, second, to supply all of our needs and third, to meet the needs of others.

I've also noticed that people with a poverty mentality aren't givers, yet they get angry when they see givers prospering and living abundant life. Don't be afraid to believe that God wants to give you abundance, because the Bible says:

"The living God, who gives us richly all things to enjoy"; "And God is able to make all grace abound toward you, that you, always having all sufficiency in all things, may have an abundance for every good work" (1 Timothy 6:17 and 2 Corinthians 9:8 NKJV).

This truth changed my life, my family, and my church and it continues to change thousands of individuals that have had enough of begging from the devil and society and have decided to exercise their rights as children of the King of the Universe.

THE BATTLE FOR YOUR MIND

Jesus Won Your Battles

I want to finish this book with a revelation that will help you in the daily battle for your mind. Do you remember the crown of thorns that they placed on Jesus' head when they mocked and beat Him? That crown has a great meaning for us today. In the Bible, thorns are synonymous with the curse. God told Adam after he sinned: *"Both thorns and thistles it shall bring forth for you, and you shall eat the herb of the field"* (Genesis 3:18 NKJV). Before man fell, the earth had no thorns in it. That curse isn't only reflected in the ground that man tills, but also in everything he does and follows him wherever he goes.

A mind without God only produces thorns and thistles. It was no accident that Jesus wore the crown of thorns. With that crown He took away the curse that was on the mind of man in which *"every intent of the thoughts of the heart was only evil continually"* (Genesis 6:5). The thorns stuck into the head of Jesus were meant to place the curse that man had on his mind on Him. The blood that He shed as a result of those thorns is what cleanses our thoughts and warns the devil that your mind was purchased by the blood of Jesus. Therefore, the devil has no more right to occupy or control your mind.

Make a decision that from now on you will live every moment for God, guarding your mind and continually depending on the Holy Spirit, so that every time you have to fight with the devil for your mind, you will end up as the *Winner*. God wants you to be able to say with Paul: *"But we have the mind of Christ"* (1 Corinthians 2:16).

A Prayer for Mental Deliverance

Merciful and Holy Father, You know my most intimate thoughts and there is no secret that I could hide from You. Right now, I realize that my mind has been influenced by people, events and the things I've experienced in life. Only you know how these things have formed and molded my character and personality. Now in the name of your Holy Son Jesus, I renounce every train of thought that isn't in line with your Word or Your plan and design for my life.

I renounce the things I've inherited from my ancestors, which were contrary to your Word. I renounce the spirit of this world that was imparted to me from birth, which doesn't have its mind on things above, but on the things of the earth. I renounce all religious training and the traditions of men that nullify the Word of God.

By the power of the Holy Spirit, I command the pulling down of every stronghold that Satan has erected in my mind. In the name of Jesus, I apply the blood of Christ to every area of my mind, so that I might be cleansed from every affect of the curse. Lord, help me to bring every thought captive to the obedience of Christ. Loose the power of Your Spirit in me, so that my mind will be used to think and do great things for Your glory. I pray all of this in the mighty name of the Lord Jesus Christ,

Amen.